xango music

first published in Great Britain in 2001
Peepal Tree Press Ltd
17 King's Avenue
Leeds LS6 1QS

ISBN 1 900 715 46 5

geoffrey philp

xango music

PEEPAL TREE

for nadia

contents

dream

i

through coal smog, armed with tear
gas, tanks necklace the hostels' muddy streets;

a soldier barks, and a swirl of egrets flash
across the sky: so many souls lost in the landslide,

like *zetoile* over cap haitien, astonished
by their own reflection, shudder to stone, fall

through the sky as shooting stars over the shanties'
pulse, flattened by thunder and *rara* drums; a sentry dulled

by white rum, a dagger to his brain, coils in the doorway,
eyes half-open, a mind dreaming awake; bullets

riddle his body, like the hooked necks of john crows
mired in the stench of carcasses, drizzle falling on dungle

heaps, their eyes fixed on gardens around the *hounfort*
when yam stalks will grasp sunlight, when a seed will break

its shell in half, when brothers are reborn, ridden
like those horses up the mountains of jacmel.

ii

and in the dream, descending from the sun, an elder,
dressed in green and kente, gold fringes, whose name
was *egum*, walked down the steps of a white aeroplane,
and i greeted him, kissed both cheeks, and told him,

"we're all here," and he replied, "are you, my son,
enjoying your life as a nomad?" then, as in all dreams,
the scene shifted to my father at my old home
who said, "life is too short, my son, to live in fear."

iii

like those birds escaping the mouth of volcanoes
i have made the journey to this strange place

that stretches its hand into the bowl of the atlantic,
a land of "waterpigs", raccoons, opossums, and alligators,

with common trees: tamarind, naseberry, trumpet tree,
to find in this wood the shape of a familiar ancestor,

some relic of the conversation between the dead
and living, to ease the load of those going ahead.

song to the loas

(for felix morriseau-leroy)

imagine how these anhingas give themselves
to the wind, riding air currents over the canal

as it turns away from the highway's hum
and the live oak's acorns falling between palmetto

fronds and poinciana's fire; or how mullets break
the surface of the water in their singular joy

that makes them one with the air; so do i hope,
when my body flames with the crotons, my *nâme*

with roots of the banyan, my little good angel,
held in faded photo albums and remembered years

later in a libation, and my star of destiny settles into its
constellation, my great good angel will find peace in *ginen*

morning jog

walkman loaded, jogging beside snake creek,
a flock of ibises, like the opening scene

of *out of africa*, rise with the rain,
their reflection multiplied on the face of the lake

as they turn towards their true path, wings, beaks
trained towards the south, their final destination,

away from rain that bends leaves of bracken
and marsh ferns parted by shadows of their wake.

but excluded from that vision, on this damp street,
men relax their hold on the chains of their pit

bulls' necks, women in sweat suits begin to zip
up their jackets, careful not to expose vanilla breasts,

and i turn up the volume, on this day of the festival of lots,
gathering rain in my hands, the thunder i have reaped.

song for christina

walking arm in arm with you away from the river
was such a gift after so many days on the road:

shifting restlessly in motel rooms from bed
to bed, pacing between the bathroom and dresser,

never finding the right groove, even after i left
the nightlight on, a reminder of the times i held

your body through fevers, mopping your forehead,
your eyes shut tight, hallucinating about ants

crawling up your legs – i worried about your future
as the t.v. blared more bad news – would you find your way?

for so many friends have given up, given in to greed,
and i know we share this passion for metaphor –

which makes me feel all the more helpless because i
can do nothing, but walk by your side.

santa fe blues

george toasts you in the pool hall as if you were dead,
and the juvvie with the tattoo (you screwed her in the back

of the 7eleven) still remembers you when she breaks
a new game – she hustles for money now instead of weed.

"miami's too big," you said and, stereo blasting, drove
2370 miles to escape the crack whores and nickel bag

freaks who fed your hunger for crack, coke, ecstasy – any drug
that would dull the ache, make you forget, leave

this city that slowly tied a noose around your neck
while you tried to ignore the insults in *merengues* –

then gave into their threats, gave into your fears,
and they branded your friends: nigger, kike, spic.

a wall of heat, like amnesia, rises off the desert in santa fe.
but *despierta,* my brother. dance to your song, "vuelvo a nacer."

mother song

enough then! you're dead, it's over.
all the beatings with electrical cords, high heeled

shoes, and, your favourite, a switch from the tamarind –
anything you could grab in moments of anger

after your husband left you for another woman;
then the poison that soured everything you touched

would eat away at your stomach as you lay in bed
naked, man-less, and horny, sweating sin,

blaming me for being born, your fucked-up life,
when all i was being was a boy, the son

of my father, the man you now hated – his name
would send you into a rage, the slow burning grief,

and you'd light a cigarette, cry into your pillow, alone.
i'd awaken with welts – the signature of your shame.

father song

back in the fifties, a high colour brown man, you'd pass
for white and often did until a family friend

strolled past the guards, dived into the deep end
of the myrtle bank hotel. the manager screamed raas,

and drained the pool, scrubbed the sides clean
of any residue of the black man who had tainted

the pool with a belly flop from top rungs and splashed
water on the thighs of young ex-pats trying to darken

their skin in the colonies. but you could never pass –
they were yours for the taking – secretaries in the office pool

eager to rise to another class, to improve the race
with mulatto children whose colour would grant access

(over their darker sisters) to parties at beverly hills.
for them to fall, you only had to brush the curls from your face.

sacagawea
(for bathsheva)

did you have to cross a continent to be free,
fighting currents, digging up camas roots, onions,

trying to read raw trails for a new direction,
pushing past gnats, mosquitoes into the prairie?

did you have to change your name to be free?
your children and ex-husband call you "birdwoman";

your journeys and truths lost in translation,
your life a part of this land, part of our memory –

for you've passed the northern ridge of the rockies,
seen the sun rise over the multi-coloured layers

of this earth, worn through time by fault lines, stress,
crossed this river that carries your old name and empties

its silt-laden load into the pacific, but for what, my sister?
i can't go any further. i'll wait at the source and bid you peace.

¿para donde va?

the mall deserted, closed for rosh hashanah;
a new year bursting through spoon-shaped petals
of lignum vitae while hassidim stumble along miami

gardens drive, *peyes* swaying in time with a prayer
of atonement – "who shall have rest and go wandering;
who shall be tranquil and who shall be disturbed" –

over the rumble of twenty-four hour laundromats,
drowning in liquid semi-vowels of spanglish, a.t.m.s
sputtering daily balances, receipts, withdrawals,

beside a seniors only condo, our refuge with other *goyim* –
hungarians, estonians lithuanians – who folded their scarves,
held their hats against the caterpillar's teeth grinding asphalt,

our dreams to gravel, chewing abandoned lots where our children
stifle their laughter and illegal *caleñas* smother their names
and answer the rude call of jitneys bustling down biscayne

boulevard; an ambulance clears its throat, throttles
through the parking lot, choked with minivans, all terrain four-
wheel drives – the chrome flashes of the highway brightening ahead.

millennium resolution

i'm stripping away all the lies before the next millennium:
lies that my father loved me more than his masonic brethren,

lies that he married my mother while she was still a virgin,
lies about blackness, about whiteness, about who i am.

for the lies are like dead weights that pull me down
into the undertow of money, culture, race and class,

distorting my features – the true reflection of my face –
so i've become something subtle and submarine.

but what will happen to me after i've stripped away
all the forms that clothe my mind with order,

old ways of thinking about myself – the *thusness* of reality?
what will i have but this naked, scarred body

that i have so despised, regarded always as other,
facing myself in the silence of unanswerable joy.

missing the mountains

it's on mornings like this that i miss the mountains
that flanked papine, hope pastures, and mona heights

in a green horseshoe – except to the west
where plains rolled into canefields of st. catherine,

then broke into bush, limestone, and cockpit
country, home to freedom fighting maroons

who taunted the british into submission.
but what's a singular freedom if not a singular debt

paid over lifetimes? what's the use of war
or exile, if after so many losses and deaths

there's no fire to live by in the circle of friends?
the sun's steady climb over mountains to meet my eyes

had the quiet certitude of a heartbeat, like breath,
not the endless horizon of the sea without end.

meditation on snake creek

fog billows over the troubled face of the canal;
a quilt of clouds, torn by a stand of pines, a tangle

of cumulus stuck in their needles, stretches over the hot
road rising in the east to the *reeb* of mallards strutting

over imaginary property lines of fulford-by-the-sea –
neighbours with new silverware and noise – down streets

with names as provisional as the ones we give ourselves,
behind houses swollen as the frayed textbooks

that line my shelves; while overhead in the frigid wind
from the west, past hasidic women, power-walking,

checking each other's pulse as if they weren't going to live
forever, a kestrel circles rat snakes through the everglades;

sand skitters over the page into the next millennium;
a stream that quenched ponce's thirst, washed mud

from the hair of tequesta, pours over my crown, neck,
chest, feet – the hard portions – and into the sap of the mangrove.

lake song

hands clasped with her grandmother, my daughter
feeds gulls and pigeons, then turns to the fish
that glide along the bottom of the murky lake.

this winter, all the ducks have fled the lake,
yet rising with the whir of sprinklers, my daughter
rushes down the paved walkway to feed the fish

that rise as if summoned by her footsteps – fish
burrow through floating plastic bottles that ring the lake –
and grandmother crumbles bagels to give my daughter

to feed the fish while they count morning glories
beside the lake where she breaks bread with my daughter.

snake creek elegies

i

the x where we now live, the marked cross hairs
where any day now i expect to see coyote, brer rabbit,

or eshu with his famous hat strolling down the street,
a real cocksman, to stir up troubles with my neighbours.

but i'm ready for him now, i've lived to have my store
of tricks and spells to ward him off – except the answer

to the prank he played on the former owners
who've left the *mezuzah* hanging over the door.

ii

this royal poinciana (planted by some cracker,
now a statistic of white flight from dade county
afraid of what miami has become –
a muddle of races, dark as the canal that runs
behind the houses, that separates *goyim*
from *hasidim)* whose branches hover
over my studio like a forgotten ancestor,
that undermines foundations of the playground,
sprouting its stem through deep
wounds in the limestone, like the web of highways
that left overtown homeless, puts out its first buds,
smothered by ash from the names mcduffie
and lozano, blooms every juneteenth through august
after andrew's baptism of homestead,
and has grown down from the sky, giving way to the tug
of gravity, still holding its fire against white clouds,
admitting itself to be a part of the landscape, despite
twisted limbs, and giving shade to my brown children.

iii

down by the bridge, water moccasins slither
through bracken and beer bottles like the advent
of a nightmare. no wonder the ancient

egyptians cowered before snakes, masters
of eternity whose fatal bite sent the victim, unaided,
to face maat and thoth, the ibis-headed god, whose beak

balanced a feather over maat's jaws, then weighed
it against the victim's heart – a life swollen with fear –
only to be swallowed by maat's brothers waiting in the dark.

iv

under the murky water, tarpons
with beards made from rusted hooks
silver glimmering in the grasses and reeds,
drawn there as naturally as those middle-aged lovers
parked in a black mustang every noon at the foot
of the bridge, regular as the tide – while her husband's
at work, and he's taken a lunch break from the office –
undress each other and obey a pull greater
than their promises; or those kids at dusk,
at the roots of the flowering dogwood, smoking
buddha, playing the dozens with dr. dre
or ice cube as background music, arguing
endlessly about who's the better deejay;
like david, paul, pat, and me, kotched
on the fence, listening to shakespeare's bass
streaming out of twin eighteen inch speakers
and augustus pablo's haunting melodica
darting between the thrashing guitars
that strained the tweeter's throat,
until some cop, like saddlehead,
would try to sneak up on us

to cart us off to jail in bright handcuffs,
but david would always sense his shadow,
and before he could tighten his dragnet,
we'd be off into the night, fluorescent
puma sweatshirts flashing in the darkness.

v

gray manatees munch river grass,
anhingas sun themselves on broken limbs,
and the muddy path around the lake doubles
like legba's riddles about opossums.

so what's left now? like the famous warrior,
his enemies slain, the kingdom restored,
he put down his bow, (useless now in the real war)
to rebuild the hearth beyond the beckoning road.

easy skanking
(for nadia)

all saturday evenings
should be like this, caressing
your thigh while reading neruda
with his odes to matilde's arms,
breasts, hair – everything about her
that made him
a part of this bountiful earth –
lilies, onions, avocadoes – that fed
his poetry the way
rain washes the dumb cane with desire
or banyans break through asphalt.
this is the nirvana that the buddha
with his bald monks and tiresome sutras
never knew – or else he'd never have left
his palace and longing bride –
the supple feel of your leg in my hands
for which i'd spin the wheel of karma
a thousand lifetimes, more

mango

hidden behind a cloister of leaves,
guarded by wasps, the flesh yields
the secret of pollen; peel the skin

with your lips, sap trickles over
your fingers; the juice smells strange
on your beard; suck through the meat,

take the stone into your mouth,
and feel the hairs tickle your tongue;
call the goats, for the season is over.

sunset at greynolds park

"weeeee," my son's scream
unhinges an egret from the sea-
grape's gnarled boughs; bitter juice
rises in my throat; his mother's station
wagon enters the parking lot filled
with minivans – young couples still naive
enough to believe in love – yet i wish it was
us swinging higher into that arc that binds me
closer than the twin poles of the swings
that span the sandbox, our space,
where our children bloodied their hands
on the jungle gym, trampled now by raccoons
awakened by the sweet stench of sapodillas;
the pups nuzzle the green mat of their mother's
fur beside broken sewer pipes that connect
the park to the bay – the poison of sudden
blooming algae coming in under an orange sky
where 747s play tag over the barrier islands
stranded in the gulf's reach toward guyana,
like our restless drive to renew ourselves;
coming in before the tug-of-war between my jeans
and his mother's skirt – my son's small arms,
like a frail spider stitching the severed space;
coming in under the fingers of mangroves
pulling the tide, the retreat of hermit crabs
under sand, pulling me closer to us, closer to we.

nature walk

to talk about these trees, lakes, rivers
is not to be deaf to all the horrors:

a brother was lynched on this flowering dogwood,
brickell's skyscrapers cataract with ash from rosewood,

the suwannee will never wash away the blood
from these states, and those deserted dirt roads,

inviting as the drawl of southern belles in leon county,
are not as innocent as they seem to be.

yet this river, subversive as its silt, overruns
its banks, stirs the rank mud, startles spoonbills, herons

and manatees in their own element, accepts complicity –
life feeding on itself – with the yellow pollen of the trees.

a song for my children

beyond the deafening roar of the highway, your mother
and i walked across the bridge down the river
where a family of five cast their lines over rocks
that jutted out of the banks covered with flowers,
lichen, silver moss, and ferns – a hovel for snakes
that slithered across the street at night into our garden.

how many times, you ask, have i cleared and weeded our garden?
when i squatted in the dirt and pulled green stems like my mother
with a crooked stick and machete in hand to chop the snakes –
all that i'd learned from that country girl who'd lived by a river
that made the earth moist and every april made lilies flower
between the spaces in the stone fence and among the rocks

that separated our land from our poorer cousins' who threw rocks
at us, and we ran for shelter behind the barbecue near the garden
of periwinkles, oyster plants, leaf-of-life, all the common flowers
that grew by the wayside, trampled by traffic, that my grandmother
rescued while carrying water on her head up from the river
that coiled around the heart of seaford town, then snaked

towards the sea where crocodiles and sea snakes
crawled out of the water and warmed themselves on rocks,
like the fabled mermaids that combed their hair – river
mumma we called them – on the sides of that watery garden
that held our family together through drought until my mother
left the country, searching for a place where her life could flower

in a different soil; so she smuggled sinkle bible, leaf-of-life, flowers
from her parents' garden, snipping the stems and watching for snakes
that wrapped around the roots. she was leaving her mother
and father in a land where men's hearts were as hard and cold as rocks
that lined the marl road; she would leave the shadow of their garden
and take the road leaving struie and follow the river

through the swamp into the sea, always wondering "how many rivers,
lord, will i still have to cross?" yet she counted the flowers
on her path, collecting as her mother had, blossoms for her own garden
that she mulched and fenced to keep away snakes
that loved the dark soil, bits of bark, and smooth rocks,
preserving the lessons she had learned from your great grandmother

that i give to you now; for our garden, too, has rocks
your mother and i found by the river where you were born, and
despite snakes in damp corners, flowers with trumpet trees this easter.

version break

(for kwame dawes)

it is the moment
in the dancehall when sweat
drips down the dawta's forehead,
miss clairol tackles sensi
swirling around the rude bwai's tam,
when everything get dread,
like just before you crash
everything slows down to speed up

                   — the version break —
when i can feel my mother's eyelashes
on my belly, smell the appleton on my father's breath —
before the pulse of the bass thuds into my chest,
and the shimmer of the high hat, seductive
as judy mowatt's voice climbing over rita's
and marcia's harmony. "i wanna, i wanna jam,
i wanna jam it with you," and the riddim unfurls,
like the world beginning, again.

drumpan chicken, kola champagne, bammy, festival and red stripe
beer at hellshire beach ; john crows wheeling over long mountain; the
sweet sensi seeping over wareika; ground doves pecking gungo peas
in the gully of elleston flats; barbed wire and grass bokkle; guinea gogs
and gorgons flashing gongs and glocks on duke street; **i need a fat
girl tonight;** peaka peow, mah jong, dominoes, ludo, allan skill cole
in the house of dread, cricket lovely cricket; belly lick, rent-a-tile,
rub-a-dub style, soldering, welding, a wha de young girl want;
cauchie, strike, roadblock, curfew, gun court; macka fat, gizadas and
tinking toe while skulling school; bleached out and black up outside
stable restaurant; wake up and live with andrew's liver salts; **i'm in
the mood. i'm feeling rude;** bruk yu ducks; panther, if you care
about life; baby mother outside the family planning clinic, pink and
black store, morin's, issa's, bundles and bundles of linen; lost in
parade with king tubby's dub; babylon on a thin wire; cows munching
in the twilight; **when i give it to you girl, you're gonna say it's
so nice;** rain bundled up like dirty laundry over stony hill; jbc, lindy
delapena, desmond hall, e.t., do it to me e.t, sweet elaine wint with
an afro like angela davis; duke reid, coxsone dodd, lee "scratch"
perry, prince buster, don drummond and skatalites; big youth, i-roy,
king stitch, scotty, u-roy; she got it, she's got it, she's got it, wow;
jolly buses and mini vans trundling through cross roads, denham
town, trench town, franklin town, shanty town to the *toom* of family
man's bass; constant spring road as slippery as rico rodriguez's
trombone; **see it dey, see it dey, fatty, so nice;** port royal sinks
into its own wickedness; pieces of eight, spanish jars, doubloons,
henry morgan, hawkins and drake; coolie baboo, chinee, syrian,
brown man, backra, every nigger is a star; anansi, tacky, paul bogle,
nanny, marcus garvey, sam sharpe, walter rodney; duppies, rolling
calves, headless horseman, who is mr. brown?, the crack of bones,
the sweat of the whip; **girl, you gonna get a lot of it; get it galore;**
my heart still beats uncha, uncha uncha, cha

a poem in two parts about alligator wrestling

i

sammy struts across the limestone soft sand
to the bounce of music from a local steel pan,

body primed and readied by years of toil,
muscles ripple with the sheen of johnson's baby oil.

sammy waits for volunteers by the hut's torch-ringed lights,
a guide ushers a woman rouged with mosquito bites.

papa, her husband, sports a mets' t-shirt, she a bronze tan,
but the look in his eyes tell you, he's a yankee man;

for his roving eye, there's nothing exotic to shoot on the tour,
they've reggaed and limboed, but for him it's been such a bore;

yet this show's different, brand new attraction, a dreadlocked tarzan,
whose only real love is to wine and grind and to marry jane;

first, he feigns left, grabs the gator's head, the squirming tail dangles
between his legs; the woman gasps and they plunge into tangled

roots; he becomes a tadpole, a beeny black comma
wriggling through her hair and into the guide's patois:

lungs on fire, he measures breath, it's a struggle for mastery,
the uneven feet of man and beast wrestle belly to belly;

minutes pass, bubbles like vowels break the surface;
she disappear and right now the jerk pork don't taste

too sweet in papa's throat when the alligator come out
with her scarf, a brief stuffed with dollars hanging from it mouth.

papa get frighten because him figure him wife was running away,
make the wrong corner and almost end up as alligator entree.

when they finally meet, they both looked sorry, yet he wouldn't agree,
that for a hundred and fifty, this was the show he wanted to see.

yet papa now swore fidelity, said he'd never again leave her side,
and she said if that if was the price, it was well worth the ride.

ii
sammy struts...

sestina for bob

it started with a silly quarrel when my lover
changed the music from dancehall – she wanted to listen to bob.
i wish all our choices were that simple – not the struggle
everyday between the open sea and the comfortable yard,
the blind hunger that disguises itself as freedom
and becomes what we most dread.

it's like when i'm listening to *natty dread,*
"bend down low" when marley's talking to a coy lover,
you know he wants her, but he still wants his freedom,
and you can imagine her outside island house as her head bobs
up and down – she knows she'll become one of the women in the yard,
but she wants the man behind the music, so why struggle?

yet for marley that was all that mattered – the struggle
to change our hearts, so when the twelve tribes in that dread
day, disgusted with the shistem, will leave yard,
and africa will open her arms like a neglected lover,
we'll find the dreamland we always wanted, the place that bob
glimpsed in the streets of trench town, searching for freedom.

but is africa the only place that we'll find our freedom?
in england, in america, in france, is it only the struggle
that will give us peace, that will help us find the place that bob
told us about in "so jah seh"? urging the faint-hearted dreads
in the heart of babylon that hated him like a spurned lover,
to never give up their hope and promised better yard;

for he never forgot that babylon tried to murder him in his own yard,
jumping over so many trench town fences to find the freedom
he never found in the sweet kisses of his contented lovers;
as he trod through i-ration – couldn't sleep because of the struggle
for redemption – the ancestors tormented him, tugged at his dreads
flowing over the stones – he could never rest as they whispered, "bob

we are here in the dark, hungry and waiting. bob, bob,
the politicians, the traitors are betraying the youth a yard,
and there's no more turning back, there's no more retreat, dread.
this time, the fatherless children must fight for their freedom,
their lives will never be their own unless you continue the struggle,
only then will their eyes soften towards each other like lovers."

it hurt too much, so i left the room when bob began *songs of freedom*,
his voice with the smell of yard spilling over the lyrics – his struggle
to convince us he would always be here, like a constant lover.

sun is shining

under a blistering sun, heat
soaks through sweat down to the bone,
another reason for cells, in their molecular
dance, to divide against themselves,
like the earliest mitosis that sculpted
my shoulders, arms – my son's round
forehead blossoming, like a harvest moon
over the horizon in his mother's uterus,
and the fear – the oldest human nightmare
that one day a harvest cycle would breed a horn
of maggots – old as abraham's desire to appease
(the twin desires of sacrifice and blood)
the god that bound him to his word, yet stayed
his hand with a bleating ram that waited,
trapped in the bush, from the first day
the earth breathed, and turned his heart
toward the mute seer whose only prophecy
was to sire his own story of creation:
to deny the dead flesh on his face,
shoulders or accept the cool gift of aloe
sprouting under the fingers of the date palms.

healing in the balm yard

i

dressed in my garbardine suit,
miami heat prickling my neck,
filled with the spirit, i'm ready to shout.

all the troubles that've followed me this week
i've thrown aside and, surrounded by the choir,
peace covers me; i take my lord's kindly yoke.

then our voices rise with the river,
and our throats swollen with suffering
we follow the lead of preacher,

our tribulations transformed into this song:
in this place, peniel, we see the face of god —
a crowd of witnesses, we join the holy throng.

ii

and when the spirit
descended on this place
after the laying on of hands,
i recognized the flap of wings,
the heaviness of incense — i had seen
this before — my tongue cleaved to the roof
of my mouth. only after in the temple
when we were raised
to be prophets in an evil land,
when we were no longer afraid
of romans and iron,
could we stand and declare
the word in our hearts;
for other men, too, had seen this

movement: the hush of candles,
the steadying flame,
then wept in their brokenness;
but we have come face-to-face
with the fire and proclaim ourselves
healed.

xango music

beside broken axles, the *pang, pang,*
pang slips under torrington bridge, climbs
over wareika into ital seasoning,
skitters over swimming pools
of beverly hills into the dub of jolly buses
grinding up cross roads, half-way-tree, liguanea
– the president meets the residents
of mona, hope pastures, and stony hill
at matilda's corner; my sister, outside
the post office, swollen eyes, swollen fingers,
sends a letter across the pond
to cousins in paris, brixton, goteburg,
asking for money cause everything's late;
behind her a veil of rain, the drip,
drip, drip of sky juice into a cheese pan
by a door that opens into a bob-wired yard;
natty dreads bubble up from carib theatre,
scene of the first feel, casting shadows left and right –
to papine, hermitage, elleston flats,
stitched from coast to cove, by a man
beating old iron into the shape of thunder.

nanny

how many more sons, she asked the elders,
were going to be sent into the jaws of the plantation
planting rattoons, then loading the green blades

into laden wagons drawn by mules with names
more dignified than theirs, more valuable
in the accountant's ledger? sons who looked

older than her father, greyed by the whip,
broken in the fields under a grudging sun.
how many more daughters, she asked the elders,

were going to be sent to pick the cotton, belly bang
with pickney for some white man's pleasure?
better to be hungry and free, than sated and chained

to work that robbed her sweat of joy.
a woman should live to see her children grow
wild like callaloo in the yard, noisier

than ducks pecking corn around the kitchen steps.
tonight, when the moon slipped behind the boughs
of the blue mahoe, leafless as she was childless,

she would fool the great house, blind them with bullets
and bandoolu, and under the cover of the wild yams
escape through limestone caverns to the green mountains.

oshun

(to michelle cliff)

this morning i could have sworn i saw oshun
rise out of the water – *she who makes her people one.*

i needed to see her this morning after james byrd junior,
our brother, was dragged to death by a truck in jasper,

texas; for i need to believe this morning – i don't want
to be a tongueless bell – i don't want to be burnt

up like a useless limb by my own simmering hate.
oshun, guardian of our dreams and our spirit,

lover of our dark hands, dark bodies, dark skin,
healer of wounds made from enemies and our weapons

aimed at ourselves, my sister, protect us in this dread
hour until anger passes – wash your coolness over my head.

paul bogle

he believed in us before we believed ourselves –
a prophet who couldn't bear to see his people starving:

the cost of flour, salt fish rising and the day rate falling.
chained without chains, slavery without slaves,

apprenticeship over, set free, but still bound to the plantation;
joined by flesh, by the church, by ties deeper than blood,

they cut the cane that slashed their backs, and distilled
sugar in vats that turned their sweat into the rum's clean

taste that slaked governor eyre's thirst, burned his throat.
climbing down the pulpit, he banded with his brothers,

"war is at us; the black skin war is at hand". they armed
themselves with sticks and cutlasses against the queen's might.

governor eyre's hand on the noose, the *onyx* in the harbour,
he left stony gut like a bridegroom to meet his bride.

homage to michael

and it may be said, when his enemies
gathered around him with their m-16s
smuggled through north coast hotels,
glocks bought in with cessnas full of coke,
when the cia, kgb, mossad, and all the intelligences
of the world backed him up in kingston,
he stood in the wind, word for word,
(this was all he had – his palms were empty).
and it could be said that with his father dead,
paul bogle dead, alexander bustamante dead,
and the island slip-sliding away beneath him,
while the *washington post* transformed him
from the son-of-a-fabian into a pawn
of fidel, opec's pipelines dried to a black
sludge, pennies trickled from the central
bank into miami coffers and tourists stayed
in their winter north, he bowed his head.
and it will be said that like any other man
he had his doubts, but instead of rattling
his staff at the clouds, deafening us with his fears,
he stepped back, admitted the mystery was too much
for one man to bear, and gave us back our lives

2/2/99
miami, florida

to an exiled poet
(to kamau brathwaite)

how could he have known,
one mo/u/rning,
mosquitoes buzzing around the anthurium's
tongue, sound systems rumbling down long
mountain, jolly buses resting on their haunches
before the tumble of another choking day
of fumes and smoke, windows dark
as *bawon samedi's* smile, and dogs barking
like smady guwane dead tonight,
how could he have known
he would hear a sound as slippery
as the dub of eastern memphis, the tracks
he had heard in marley's *chekeh, chekeh,*
chekeh, the jazz of new orleans, the hip hop
of brooklyn, the pop, pop, pop of bullets
searching for a victim, someone walking
through dew like the wind on the sea-
grapes' leaves and eyes like big head
spliffs? how could he have known,
after he was gagged and hog-tied with x-
tension and telephone cords, after he had stared
down the sceptre of xango at his temple
in the land of dis – like he was still
in the hold of some slaver bound for the coast
of barbados, human stench rising in his nostrils –
while his sister was held outside with machetes,
forced to crawl on her belly like a worm
in the dungle towards breaklight
that only mongoose can see, that he would clear
his way through the cavernous limestone and mud,
rise and eat the unleavened wheat
and awaken, sated with the date palm's wine,
his beard covered with honeycombs?

history lessons from my father:

i walter rodney

my father preached that rodney had tried to poison
the water at mona reservoir, that he'd led

a black power revolt at the university against red
people like us, and old nayga like him would soon

have the whole island in a race war
like the one they had in watts – at least

he could scuffle to miami, hide from white
heat, and knights of the imperial order.

and when rodney died, (assassinated by babylon) –
he was, by then, an asterisk in my schoolboy's

books written by his former students – i was no longer
garroted by school ties or colours of murray or cowper

house, skanking in the chapel to big youth or scotty,
my father's will defeated by his quiet revolution.

ii white witch

"nothing worse than a black man betrayed"
he told my sister, sat back, put down a smudged

copy of *the white witch of rose hall*, then told *his* tale,
for we knew nothing about the stories of annie hall

who used obeah to bind men to her waist, who led
eager slaves to her bed with the smell of blood

veiled under the dun magic of her skin,
mesmerized the weak with her potions

and perfumes, and murdered three husbands,
then planted three coconuts as headstones,

and was eventually strangled by her black overseer
who wrapped her tongue around her neck for being a whore,

and as they grappled him away from *his* woman's stained bed,
he grinned and grinned all the way up the scaffold.

carib stew

first, you need a pot or basin
large enough to bury
the ingredients under salt
water; throw in the cheapest bones:
africans, indians (three continents),
chinese, lebanese, the odd jew.
add to the stock: english beef, scotch
bonnet peppers, a smack of spanish
parsley, irish potatoes and slivers of french
bread; bring to a boil with colonialism,
capitalism, democratic socialism,
and soon islands of froth, small
as grenada, should be scooped
off the top and the bones removed,
for if left on the bottom for too long,
they will ferment into a riot of flavour
too strong for american tastes.
(the jawbones of goats, round
as the stones on the south side
of cuba, should be never be used.)
stir well, to the consistency of molasses,
and simmer for five hundred years.
for best results, serve while hot!

song of the narwhals

beach umbrellas tremble from the shock of twin
blasts in the bulkheads of the *ocean alley,* sunk
deliberately, as it heaves its stern in the air –
like the grunt of a grampus – before the forecastle
sinks off the coast of islamorada to become part
of the coral reef, a haven for dolphin and parrot fish
poking the cold gunwale, scaffold of rock;
seaweed, tightening its green noose, coils
around the hull, around cabin windows,
round as a *balsero's* necklace, or watery eyes
of groupers caught in nets of fishing boats
trawling into the keys before sea gulls break
from their pattern to news of another shock –
before the hoarse atlantic, home to these whales
who begin their journey off silver bank
up to plymouth, can begin its usual elegy
for these small boats that set out from west end
on the cycle of waves, back and forth, ribbed
like the *hero,* packed to its helm with ashanti,
ibo, coromantee, the cries from underneath like ahab's
whale, or lowell's mad cry at nantucket, heard
in the ear of a conch, propped on the side of a tap-tap
on a flooded street of port-au-prince, where little boys
guide their paper boats down gullies and into the sea.

harbour light

stowed under the wing of a dc 10,
my nephew, oscar, above clouds
that stretch like a damp page
across the horizon, writes
his own passage with 250 other
marines, up from panama,
who made the basin safe
for the revolution of roulettes,
the usual red against black, the clean
sweep of haitian janitors in the hotel's
lobby, after the jump-up and limbo
of tourists' bath in a sea that smoothes
volcanoes to pebbles, an ellipsis of islands
barricaded by the unfinished parenthesis
of cuba, a crescent moon, a scar as small
as manacles on the *henrietta marie*
with its chessboard of light in the hold:
pawn takes queen to the sound of quadrilles,
squares dancing a jig to the scream
of bagpipes that once resisted the needling fife,
scottish brogues buried under english
vowels in an amnesia as complete as the o
he begins his name and the plane heads north.

ii
as the plane descended, barrier islands
small as duckweed – like blotches on an impressionist's

canvas – gave way to islands of the south, remnants
of an earlier catastrophe, their ridges rising like carapaces

49

over the atlantic's broken rim — a geologist's disturbed
dream: a ring of volcanic peaks jutting into rain clouds,

like pyramids of chac mol demanding the young
for the gift of rain that waters the cane; bananas, ripped

by the other god, huracan, smoldering over the foam
where a hermit crab with his house on his back,

his secret of survival, turns away from the glare
of headlights, scavengers on the lookout for the green

fat of turtles, pirates mining salt, selling sand for pearls,
plundering sunken slavers and coral headstones: coolie,

nigger, indian, conky joe, welded to limestone by fingers
of mangrove into the crown of islands that we call home.

shabine's children

(to derek walcott)

after rain pelted the australian pines,
we followed meandering paths along the canal

choked with twigs, slivers of sawgrass bobbing
over currents, around boys casting their fishing lines

into dark water rushing under the bridge to the mouth
of the river, gateway for our fathers, absented by exile

or death that visited you so early, while you struggled
through good and bad marriages, dismal affairs splashed

in tabloids, in *time,* eager to print every indiscretion, brand
you with calumnies from which no prize could ever save you

because of the war the of blood in your veins, more rancorous
than the fires that swallowed troy or castries, followed by rants

of sycophants and jesters. only a fool would remain
after the fetes and bobol to trace paths in the ash, dust,

rubbish – like the wanderings of telemachus through forests;
and while the island's heat prickled your scalp, terns

and egrets stalked their prey, then congealed into a single
metaphor, more real than light reflected off the harbour,

a wash of colours as translucent as the crests of waves
slipped out the headland and into the atlantic.

i had to leave a little girl (version)

you were the one who closed that door.
you were the one torn by your own guilt,
so tortured by your imaginings that you swore
we'd never lie together again, sharing sweat
in a bed that we knew was all too sweet,
despite our duties and obligations; but we were
one with our passion, which we had in moments
in a time when that was *all* we knew was sure.
so don't think any less of yourself then or now:
your breast in my mouth, your legs around my waist,
my hands on your thighs, was that all just for show?
when we warmed each other by our bodies' glow,
tangled in covers, the heat rising off my chest,
did you really think i could stay away from your pillow?

countdown

weaving behind a drunk driver on 135th, cluster
bombs poised to hit baghdad, george moses horton's
rhythms in double-dutch on the streets of opa-locka,

burning spear on the dashboard, scoping out
the yellow women with red eyes who share their stuff
around the hood to pay florida plunder and loot,

(for the men they leave, a year from now, will be as yellow,
cold, and sweaty as they are, broken like the blighted palms
along the boulevard: spines split by the virus that passes

through the projects – not enough to kill outright,
but enough to poison the sap, lay the branches low,
until they finally wither away); where triplets

in the middle of the street, kools stuck behind their ears
before they graduate, become marlboro men, dare oncoming
cars like the paper men with *herald* headlines: "one in three

black men denied the vote" – but these boys dodge with less care,
and the drunk driver seems determined to reduce the miraculous
to the mundane, so i cut in front, barely making it on the inside,

leaving the smallest stranded on the unbroken yellow line,
breaking the law for a greater law, remembering, even if they've
forgotten, even when they think black boys don't count.

bob marley in the day care center

i first glimpsed him, the smile,
as he played peek-a-boo in the communal playpen
inside the young president's club, mt. sinai,
after circle time with the toddlers, reading
real-life stories of heroes whose only weapons
were words aimed at the dragon's heart,
(they stared, transfixed, at the sound
uncoiling from his mouth like smoke).
he placed them gently on their blue cots
(while the older kids built castles with blocks,
unsteady as jericho's wall to the rastaman's song),
then retreated to the infants' area to sponge-bathe
the early risers. he'd burned through life so fast
he'd never really grown accustomed to this
human softness — no longer the hard, bitter seed
that couldn't wait to shatter its shell,
like the eucalyptus pods that fell
on the playground where he'd decided,
almost a lifetime ago, this time he'd take it slow.

poltergeist or the *duende's* gift

if only sleep or a good night's rest
could absolve my many betrayals:
retreating when i should have stepped forward,
retiring when i should have charged ahead,
for ghosts keep tumbling into bed with me,
they grow arms and legs and poke and kick
and jab all through the night, and i'm left
standing naked in the bathroom mirror,
battered and bruised in the sunlight, wondering,
how did it come to this? why have i allowed this
to go on for so long? and when i leave,
they pluck springs in the mattress,
rip pillowcases with their teeth, scatter
strands of hair on the night table, bump
photographs of happier times until they hang
lopsidedly on the walls, their edges bent
or broken, the glass stained with soot;
then they rearrange the furniture, so the troubles
i come home to look different, but are the same
tussled sheets and torn comforters. i never sleep
in the same bed twice.

a psalm

by the mouth of the miami river
where we wept under the freedom tower,
with the homeless outside camillus house,
the poor in the sweatshops of little haiti,
the huddled masses under the turnstiles
of the allapattah train station –
for we have put away our *kettes*, hung them
on limbs of the gumbo limbo
withering from the curse of *restaveks*
on a far atlantic coast – how can we sing
when we pass through these walls
medallioned with names from above the hold,
with the hunger of ghosts for songs
beyond the whip?
and if i forget you, o kingston, when i stood
on matilda's corner and everyone knew my name,
let my hand forget its skill on the drum & bass;
if i fail to love you more than my highest joy –
watching the streetlights at dusk turn on,
one-by-one, like peenie wallies over wareika –
let me never sing again!

smoke screen

satellites gone awry, the television snowed,
except for the sure and faithful t.b.n.
whose frost-haired preacher promises fire

for sinners like me, cursed with the sin
of canaan – too proud to submit to the grey
slate of his eyes, too humble to admit the grace

we share with the burst of rain that skitters
across a graveyard of cypresses, barely
enough to wash the blackened limbs blasted

thin of their barks by summer wildfires
along alligator alley, then south to the edge
of the everglades where a heron interrogates

a snake, (and failing, it passes through the hooked
neck – the paradox we share: the necessity of death,
the inevitability of love), then to a green field

where my mother has become a live oak,
spears of st. augustine beside the smell of wood
smoke lifting into a sky barred with wisps of smoke.

florida garden

to hear the way they tell it,
you'd think that we didn't have the right
to stand on this ground, hallowed
by the blood of all the undone, white
black, indian, pressed down by the hooves
of night riders, sprouting like kudzu
around the lakes of our state, but my mother
and i own a plot of land in orlando
where we've planted something older
and dearer than this cassava root that grips
the limestone rock and squeezes water
up the brittle stem, where her grandchildren
play ring-around-the-roses, and its leaves span
the southern cross rising above alpha centauri.

tong-len: a variation

breathe in
the blows, beatings, scars
from your father, mother, police
for not being the dream they expected

hold

breathe in
the laughter, betrayals, infidelities
of your lovers, girlfriends, one-night stands,
for pretending to be someone you weren't

feel the burn

breathe in
the curses, taunts, intimidation
from your friends, teachers, your country
for not being white enough, bright enough, black enough...

the slow fire spreads across your chest

breathe in
the dark heavy toxins that choke the light of your body
that radiate out from your stomach in a web of pain

b r e a t h e   o u t

this poem

everglades litany
(for nadia)

and blessed be the morning star in arms of gumbo limbo
blessed be the sun on cruciform wings of anhingas
blessed be the wind where ospreys and black vultures ride
blessed be zebra butterflies on crowns of tamarind
blessed be lightning on spires of royal palms.
blessed be wildfires that temper berries of green hawthorn
blessed be hurricanes that tear the bark of tallowwood and bay-cedars
blessed be bracken and wild olives huddled by salt marshes
blessed be august heat that rasps the throat of morning glories
blessed be panthers and deer hiding behind a screen of leatherwood
blessed be brown pelicans grunting in mangroves after thunderstorms
blessed be the evening star over aisles of magnolias
blessed be barred owls cooing by swamps and hardwood hammocks
blessed be june beetles dusting pollen off their backs in the damp air
blessed be woodstorks and spoonbills wading through resurrection ferns
blessed be chanterelles, their yellow plumes rising from oak and pine
blessed be the moon ripening with pond apples on the banks of canals
blessed be dew and mist, fog and hail, falling on blades of sugar cane
blessed be loggerhead turtles lumbering past the thorns of anemones
blessed be, blessed be all that move, live, and breathe on the edge of these lakes
blessed be, blessed be...

glossary

anhingas	waterfowl native to florida
balsero	cuban rafter
bawon samedi	loa of the dead and cemeteries
bobol	corruption
caleñas	women from cali, colombia
despierta	(spanish) wake up!
duende	lorca's term for mischievous spirits
egum	(portuguese) revered ancestor
eshu or legba	deity of the crossroads in vodun/yoruba cosmology
ginen ·	the world of the dead for new world africans
goyim	yiddish word for gentiles
gumbo limbo	hardwood hammock native to florida and many southern states
hounfort	vodun temple
kettes	drums of African origin
kudzu	a parasitic weed
loas	a spirit or deity in vodun cosmology
mcduffie and lozano	districts where riots took place in miami
merengues	a form of music/dance common to central america
mezuzah	a sacred talisman for observant jews which is nailed to the threshold of the front door
nâme	spirit of the flesh in vodun cosmology
oshun	female deity of streams and rivers in yoruba cosmology
peyes	earlocks worn by hasidim
rara	dance festival occurring in the spring
restavek	child labourer in haiti
sacagawea	native american guide on lewis's and clark's expedition

she who makes her people one	an excerpt from "i tie-all-my-people-together" by michelle cliff in *the land of look behind* (firebrand, 1985)
tequesta	first nation people native to florida
tong-len	buddhist meditation technique
vuelvo a nacer	(spanish) i am reborn
waterpigs	from *man and his symbols* by c. g. jung (doubleday, 1964)
white witch of rose hall	novel by jamaican writer h.g. de lisser
xango/ shango	the yoruba deity of storms and thunder
zetoile	star of destiny in vodun cosmology

give thanks to jeremy poynting and hannah bannister of peepal tree press for all their help over the years; erika waters and *the caribbean writer* for publishing my earliest and latest poems: "sunset at greynolds park," "carib stew," "xango music," "shabine's children," and "to an exiled poet" were first published in *the caribbean writer*; obsidian III for publishing "song for my children" and version break"; kwame dawes for deepening my understanding of reggae; colin channer for broadening my knowledge of reggae; mestre itaoman, baba oberefun si okojumide of círculo de estudos umbandísticos, for his kind help with the designs and his guiding knowledge of umbanda; jillian daniel and the miami-dade cultural art affairs; penny thurer and diane thiel of the miami bookfair international; josett peat of miami-dade community college who continues to look out for me; and my family, nadia, anna, christina, and andrew — one love, one art.

also by geoffrey philp

florida bound   isbn 0 948833 82 3, 1995, £5.95

for those who believe that the caribbean starts at miami, geoffrey philp's *florida bound* establishes this quirk of geography. In the journey of these poems, leaving jamaica and arriving in miami, philp meets the new blueness of "florida waters", the traffic, the interstate, with his heritage of lyric language. his poems are as vibrant and diverse as miami where "each street crackles with dialects/ variegated as the garish crotons". miami, albeit citified, becomes just one more island with all that is good, bad and potentially violent, beset by the same sea, same hurricanes, and "mangroves lashed sapless by the wind".

philp's poems wander through bedrooms and along the waterfronts of that perceptive land accessible only to poets, only to those who can pull the day through dawn fog to the delicate "breath of extinguished candles".

carrol b. fleming *the caribbean writer*

hurricane center   isbn 1 900715 23 6, 1998, £6.99

el niño stirs clouds over the pacific. flashing tv screens urge a calm no one believes. the police beat a slouched body, crumpled like a fist of kleenex. the news racks are crowded with stories of pestilence, war and rumours of war. the children, once sepia-faced cherubim, mutate to monsters that eat, eat, eat. you notice a change in your body's conversation with itself and in the garden the fire ants burrow into the flesh of the fruit.

these poems stare into the dark heart of a world where hurricanes, both meteorological and metaphorical, threaten you to the last cell. but the sense of dread also reveals what is most precious in life, for the dark and the accidental are put within the larger context of season and human renewal and the possibilities of redemption and joy.

uncle obadiah and the alien   isbn 1 900715 01 5, 1997, £6.99

"if dickens were reincarnated as a jamaican rastaman, he would write stories as hilarious and humane as these. uncle obadiah and the other stories collected here announce geoffrey philp as a direct descendant of bob marley: poet philosophizer, spokesperson for our next new world".

robert antoni, winner of the 1992 commonwealth writers prize

from the first word of the first story of this comic and touching collection, philp lifts me out of my world and drops me into the world of his charming, beleaguered and compelling characters. *uncle obadiah and the alien* is one of those rare treasures, a book you can't put down and won't ever forget.

john dufresne, author of *louisiana power and light*

64